Red Puppy

Story by Annette Smith
Illustrations by Lisa Simmons

Toys for sale

2

The teddy bears
are in the basket.

The rabbits
are in the basket.

The dolls
are in the basket.

Toys for sale

4

Red Puppy

is in the basket, too.

Look!

The teddy bears

are **not** in the basket.

8

Look!

The rabbits

are **not** in the basket.

Look!

The dolls

are **not** in the basket.

Toys
for sale

12

Red Puppy is in the basket.

Red Puppy is **not** happy.

Here comes a little girl.

The little girl is looking at Red Puppy.

The little girl is happy.

Red Puppy

is happy, too.